COLEY BEAR'S BLUE-TASTIC DAY!!

BY: SHELLEY SMITH ADAMS

Dedication

I dedicate this book to my Coley Bear whom always finds a way to keep me on my toes!

It was a quiet morning. The sun peeked
through the windows as Cole sat on the
sofa watching his favorite cartoon
character painting on the TV.

Cole had a thought . . . I want to paint too!
So, Cole tiptoed over to the craft cabinet
and saw the FINGERPAINT!

Red. Yellow. Green. And Cole's favorite . . .
BLUE! He grabbed the blue paint and
tiptoed happily back to the sofa.

BLUE!!!

He managed to get the paint open,
then dipped ONE finger in.
Then TWO.
Then his WHOLE HAND.

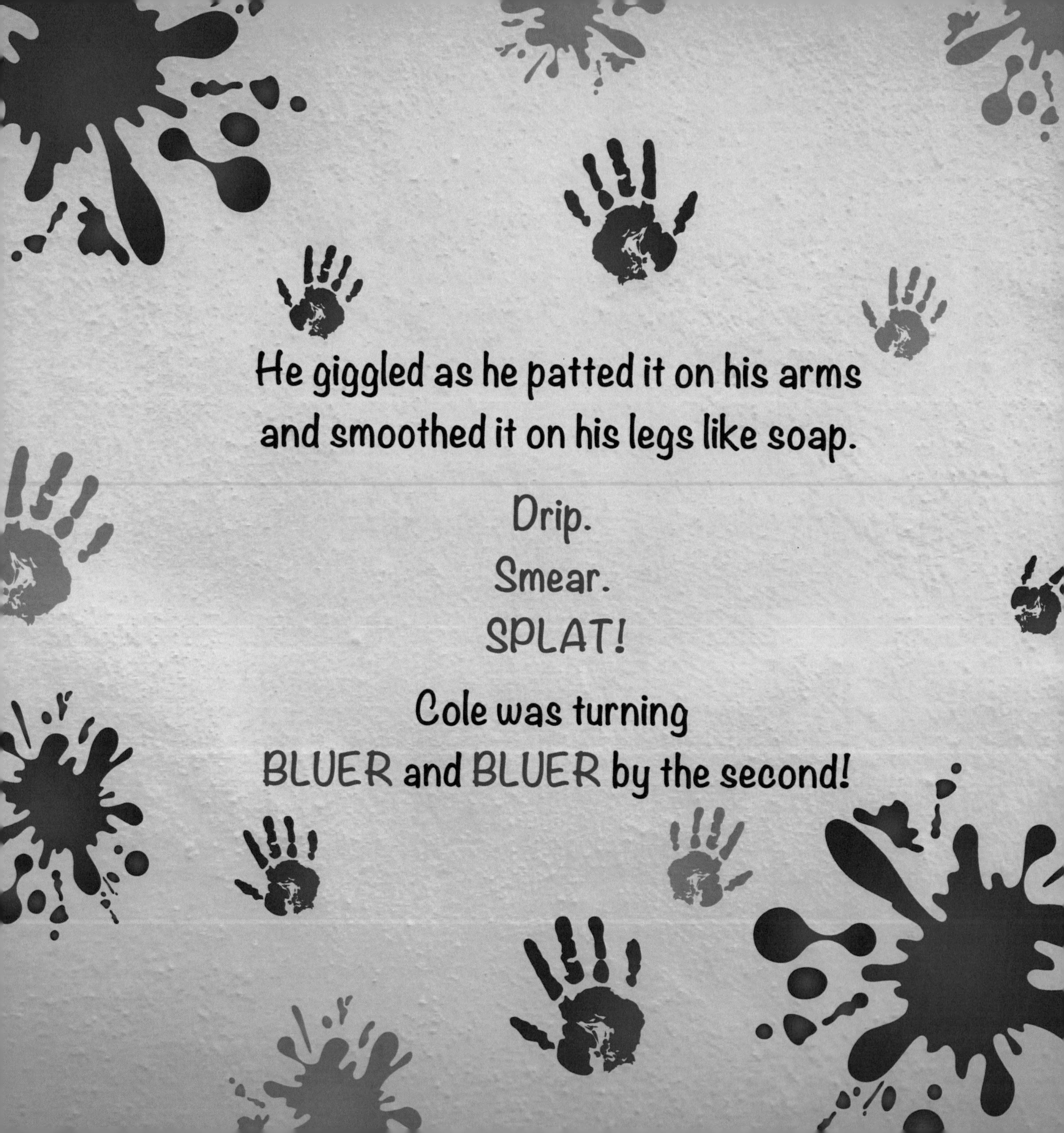

He giggled as he patted it on his arms
and smoothed it on his legs like soap.

Drip.

Smear.

SPLAT!

Cole was turning
BLUER and BLUER by the second!

Ryleigh walked into the room, her eyes
went wide. Mommmmm!!! You might
want to come and look at this!
COLE IS BLUE!

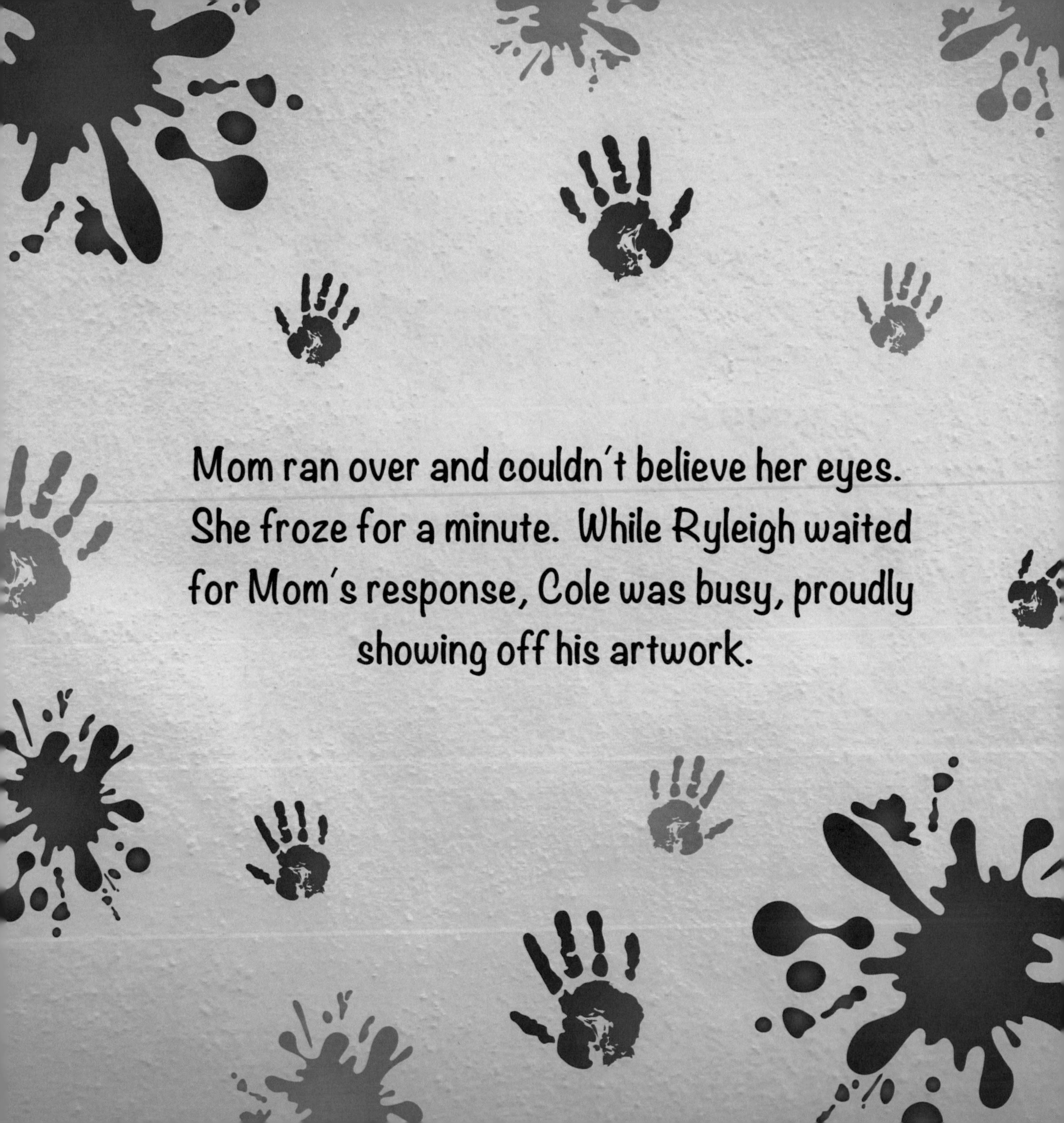

Mom ran over and couldn't believe her eyes.
She froze for a minute. While Ryleigh waited
for Mom's response, Cole was busy, proudly
showing off his artwork.

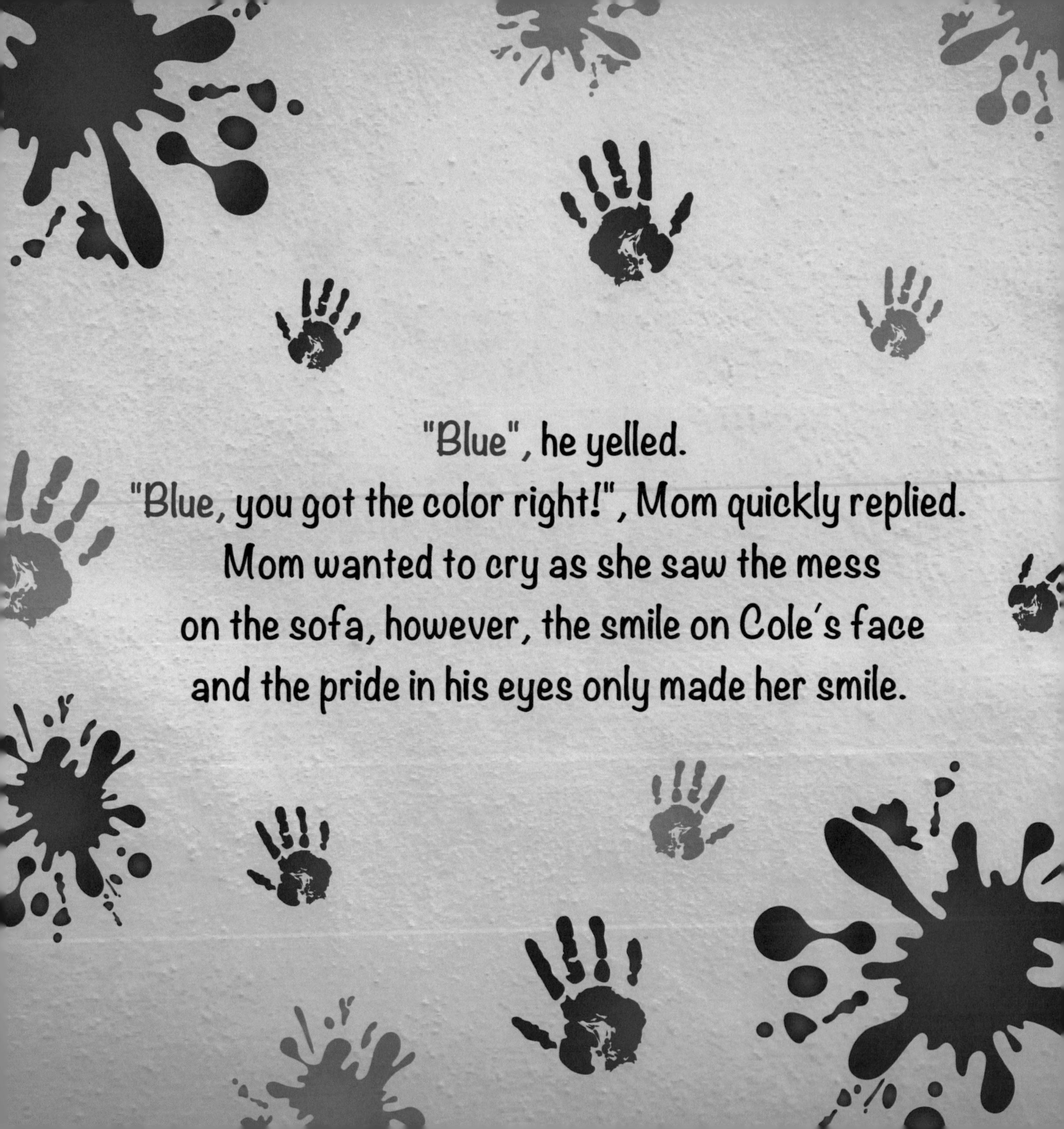

"Blue", he yelled.
"Blue, you got the color right!", Mom quickly replied.
Mom wanted to cry as she saw the mess
on the sofa, however, the smile on Cole's face
and the pride in his eyes only made her smile.

"C'mon Cole", says Mom, "Let's go take
a bath!"
"YAY!", Cole responded, as Ryleigh giggled in
the background.

Cole asked Ryleigh, "Good job?",
With a smile on her face Ryleigh replied, "Yes Cole, you
did a good job, but maybe next time,
let's paint on paper!"

Thank goodness for Daddy.